Contents

Some words are shown in bold, **like this**.
You can find them in the glossary on page 22.

How do computers work?

Computers can do many complicated things. They follow **instructions** to complete **tasks**.

Computers only do what they are told. People provide the instructions.

What are programs?

A program is a set of **instructions** that a computer follows. Computers need programs for every **task** they do.

Programs allow us to **surf** the internet, learn new things or even play games. Computers could not do anything without programs.

What is code?

Computer programs are written in code. A computer's basic language is called "machine code".

Machine code is a series of the numbers "0" and "1". It is a language you can learn like any other.

What is coding?

Giving a computer a set of step-by-step **instructions** is called "coding".

Programmers write a set of instructions in code that humans can understand. The computer then turns these instructions into machine code.

What is coding like?

Coding tells a computer what to do. These **instructions** can be as simple as "wait 5 seconds" and "play sound".

Computers only do what they are told.
They cannot think for themselves.

What is an algorithm?

An **algorithm** is a list of coding steps for a computer program. Coding steps must be in the correct order for a program to work.

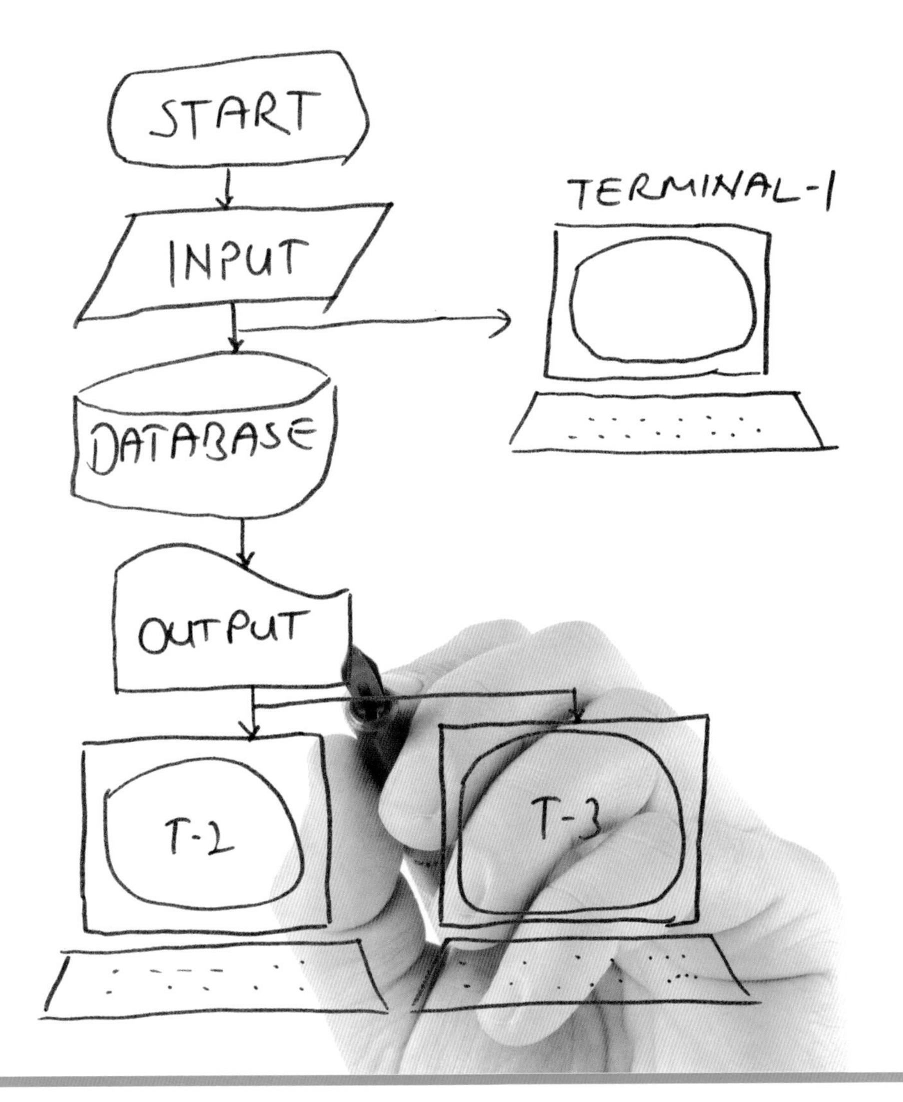

Programmers often draw a **diagram** of their algorithm. This helps them make sure the steps are in order.

What are some coding languages?

There are many coding languages. Each one is used to create different types of programs.

Javascript

Games and websites are types of programs. Some common coding languages are Scratch, Python, Java, C, PHP and Javascript.

How are coding languages different?

Each coding language has its own rules. The rules say which words and numbers should be used in a code language.

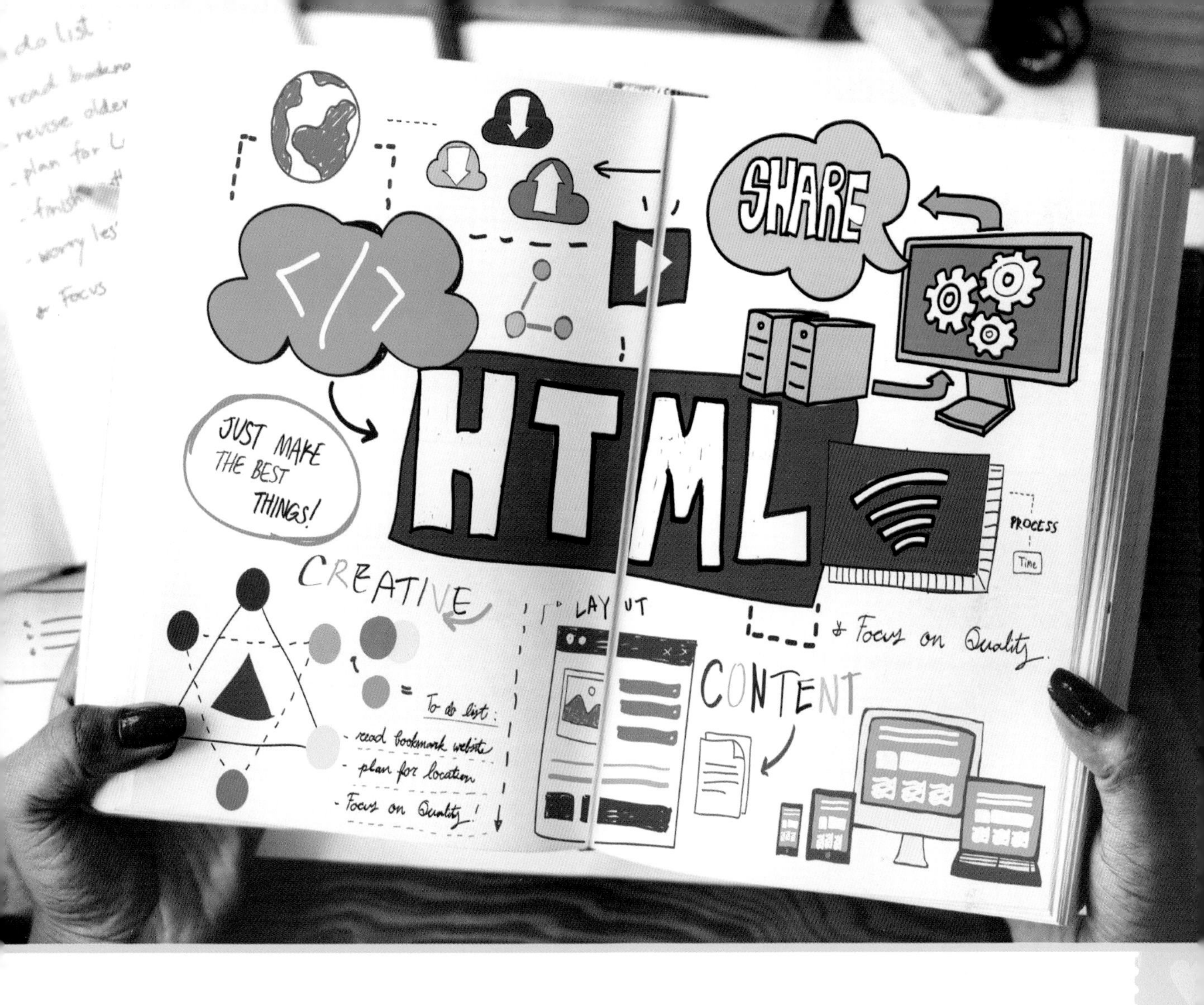

Programs will not work if the wrong words or numbers are used. Code can look strange at first. But many coding languages are easy to learn.

How do I become a programmer?

There are many ways to become a **programmer**. Your school or community centre may teach coding classes. You can also learn from books and the internet.

Ask an adult to help you try the coding websites at the end of this book.

Glossary

algorithm a list of steps a programmer gives a computer to perform a task or solve a problem

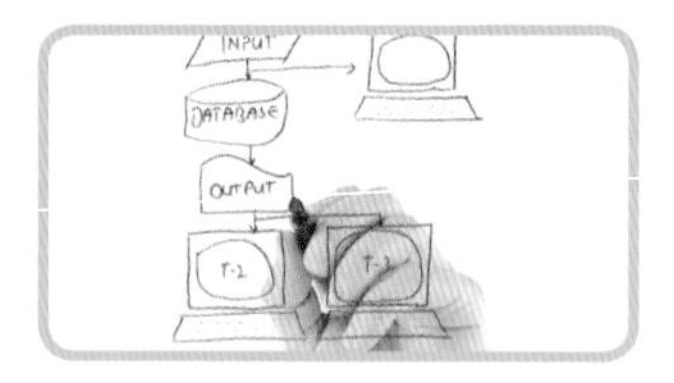

diagram simple drawing that shows how something works

instruction command or order telling something or someone to do something

programmer person who writes computer programs

surfing moving from website to website on the internet to look for something

task piece of work to be done

Find out more

Books

Computer Coding Made Easy, Carol Vordeman (DK, 2014)

Lift-the-Flap: Computers and Coding, Rosie Dickens (Usborne, 2015)

Understanding Programming and Logic (Understanding Computing), Matthew Anniss (Raintree, 2016)

Websites

moshi.kano.me/#
This Kano website lets kids code their own Pong game.

uk.code.org/learn
This Code UK website provides simple coding tutorials, including building a Star Wars galaxy.

www.bbc.co.uk/guides/zqnc4wx
This BBC website explains simple coding for young learners.

Index